THE ROAD WARRIORS
PRAYER JOURNAL

TO ....

FROM ....

DATE ....

#RoadWarriorJournal

📷 @NewHopeRBC + @NotYoGrandMaMasBibleStudy

📘 @NewHopeRBC + @NotYoGrandMaMasBibleStudy

🖱 www.NewHopeRBC.com

THE ROAD WARRIORS PRAYER JOURNAL

Copyright © 2025 by D Nicole Williams

All rights reserved.

No portion of this publication may be reproduced, distributed, or transmitted in any form or by any means, including photocopying, recording, or other electronic or mechanical methods, without the prior written permission of the publisher, except in the case of brief quotations embodied in critical reviews and certain other noncommercial uses permitted by copyright law.

For permission requests, email the publisher, addressed "ATTN: Permissions" at the following: NewHope@NewHopeRBC.com

Bulk discounts are available on quantity purchases by associations, corporations, and others for business, educational and ministry use. For details, contact the publisher at the address above.

ISBN: 978-1-942650-56-0

MY ROAD WARRIOR PRAYER

MY ROAD WARRIOR VISION

OWN MY OWN
magic

add photo here

add photo here

add photo here

take a peek at my vision

WHERE TO
WHERE TO
WHERE TO
HERE TO
WHERE TO
WHERE TO
WHERE
WHERE
WHER
WHI
WHI
WHERE
WHERE TO
WHERE TO
WHERE
WHERE TO

9

add photo here

Adventure is worthwhile

WITH AGE, COMES WISDOM.

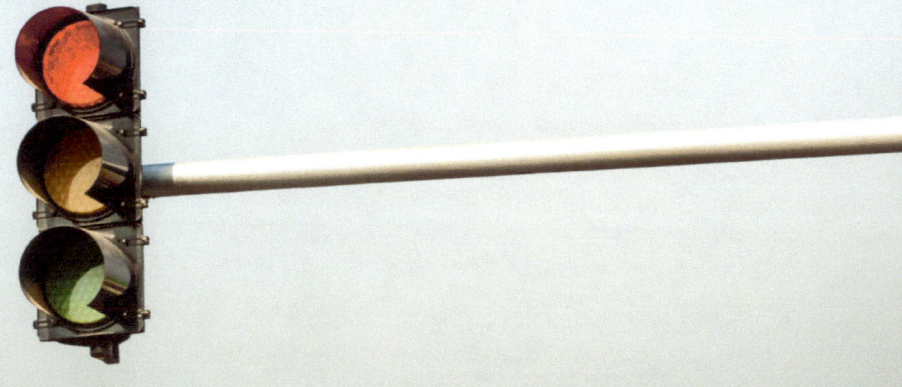

WITH TRAVEL,
COMES UNDERSTANDING.

WORK *save* TRAVEL

—

REPEAT

PRAY ABOUT TRAVEL BUDGETS

You don't have to be rich to travel well

Add life to your days,
NOT DAYS TO YOUR LIFE.

where to:

destination

IF YOU WENT TO _____

what kind of souvenirs would you buy?

1

2

3

my dream life is calling

WHERE TO WHERE TO WHERE TO WHERE TO WHERE TO WHERE TO WHERE TO WHERE TO WHERE TO WHERE TO WHERE TO WHERE TO

What was my best trip?

6
prayers
for travel
with
friends

31

3 *prayers* for travel with

pray now!

33

top 4 prayers FOR RESTFUL Vacation Options

1

2

3

SMILE FOR LIFE
NOT ONLY FOR THE PHOTO

To my mind, the greatest reward and luxury of travel is to be able to experience everyday things as if for the first time, to be in a position in which almost nothing is so familiar it is taken for granted.

BILL BRYSON

LIFE DOESN'T END AFTER SUNSET

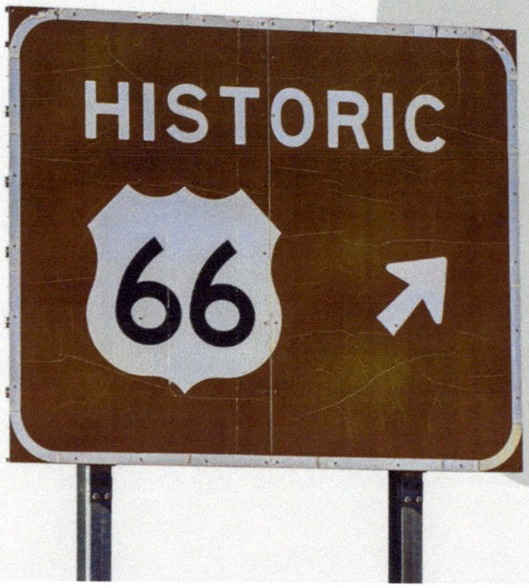
HISTORIC
66

To travel is to follow your bliss

Dare to live
the life you've always wanted

pray more

about

REMINDER:

REMINDER:

- TAKE BREAKS
- TAKE VACATIONS
- ENJOY LIFE

add photo here

All you need to know is that *it's possible*

A GOOD TRAVELER

HAS NO FIXED PLANS
AND IS NOT INTENT ON ARRIVING

> The man who goes alone can start today;
> but he who travels with another must wait till
> that other is ready.
>
> Henry David Thoreau

PRAY NOW PRAY NOW PRAY NOW PRAY NOW

three PRAYERS for Girl's Trips

FIVE PRAYERS
when traveling with friends

What are some of the benefits of TRAVELING WITH A GROUP?

WE WANDER FOR
DISTRACTION
**BUT
WE TRAVEL FOR
FULFILLMENT**

FIVE PRAYERS
for traveling with my spouse

add photo here

add photo here

61

Journey with God in Prayer

STOP BEING AFRAID OF WHAT COULD GO WRONG AND FOCUS ON WHAT COULD GO RIGHT

my favorite places for
travel in the next year

NOW on the list:

Why do I travel?

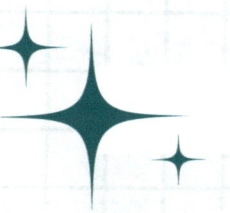

So that I can come back home.
So that I can see the place I came from with new eyes and extra colors.
And the people back home see me differently, too.
Coming back to where I started is not the same as never leaving.

— Terry Pratchett

SOMETIMES THE DIRTIEST ROADS
CAN LEAD TO

the most beautiful things

I like different places.
I like any places that isn't here.

Edna Ferber

Traveling is always a good idea

DO NOT FOLLOW WHERE THE PATH MAY LEAVE. GO INSTEAD WHERE THERE IS NO PATH AND LEAVE A TRAIL.

Home is where you park it

SOMETIMES YOU FIND YOURSELF IN THE MIDDLE OF NOWHERE

SOMETIMES IN THE MIDDLE OF NOWHERE YOU FIND YOURSELF

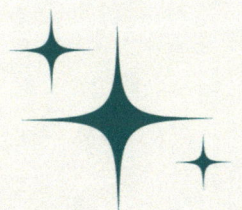
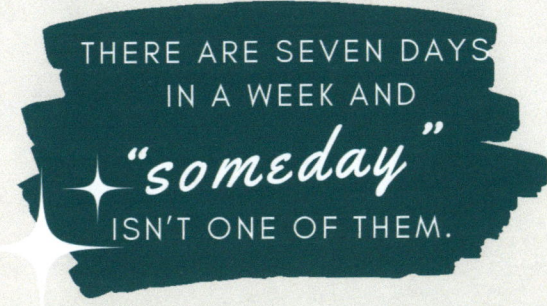

THERE ARE SEVEN DAYS IN A WEEK AND *"someday"* ISN'T ONE OF THEM.

@NewHopeRBC + @NotYoGrandMaMasBibleStudy

 @NewHopeRBC + @NotYoGrandMaMasBibleStudy

 www.NewHopeRBC.com

What you've done becomes the judge of what you're going to do — especially in other people's minds.

When you're traveling, you are what you are right there and then. People don't have your past to hold against you.

No yesterdays on the road.

William Least Heat Moon

#RoadWarriorJournal

www.ingramcontent.com/pod-product-compliance
Lightning Source LLC
Chambersburg PA
CBHW041915230426

43673CB00016B/411